D0729106

FIND AN OLD GORILLA

PATHWAYS THROUGH THE JUNGLE
OF BUSINESS AND LIFE

Bert Thornton

ISBN: 978-1-4834-3724-8 (sc)
ISBN: 978-1-4834-3723-1 (e)

Library of Congress Control Number: 2015914104

Lulu Publishing Services rev. date: 9/21/2015

CONTENTS

ABOUT THE AUTHOR

Albert S. (Bert) Thornton

Bert Thornton is a 1968 graduate of the Georgia Institute of Technology, where he attended on a full football scholarship. He spent two years as an artillery officer in the United States Army, serving a tour with the 5th Battalion, 2nd Artillery in South Vietnam.

Upon separation from the service, Bert worked as a systems analyst and salesman in NCR's IT Division and in 1971, he joined Waffle House as a manager trainee. Four years later, Bert became a vice president.

He spent forty years shaping careers (including his own) as Waffle House grew from a few southern restaurants to the iconic national presence it enjoys today.

As President and Chief Operations Officer in 2004, Bert felt his number one priority was the development of quality leaders and leadership skills within the Waffle House management team.

In recent years, Bert has focused his message on emerging leaders from many other companies, educational institutions and business associations. Thousands of students, mentors and business people of all ages have heard and benefited from his "Success Tactics" presentation.

Bert's driving motivation is the age-old adage: "When the student is ready, the teacher will appear." The overwhelmingly positive feedback from his presentations over the years confirms that Bert did appear at the correct time for hundreds of men and women who are successful leaders today in business and many other venues.

In 2015, Bert is Vice Chairman Emeritus of Waffle House, Inc., one of the largest 24-hour restaurant chains in the world.

And, yes, if you are a Waffle House fan, he is the Bert of Bert's Chili.

A PARABLE

It's what you learn after you know it all that counts.
—John Wooden

Once upon a time, at the edge of a jungle not so very far away, there were two young gorillas equal in strength, agility and desire for achievement. They shared a similar dream to climb to the top of a distant mountain that was surrounded and guarded by a difficult jungle.

One day the two young adventurers decided to pursue their dream. Together, they left home to head for the jungle's edge and the mountain beyond. By chance, they passed a band of old gorillas in a clearing at the edge of the village. When the young gorillas boasted of their quest, the elder chief of the band cautioned that they would greatly benefit from the voice of experience. The first young gorilla chided the elder chief, believing himself to be strong and invincible. He did not want to slow down and departed immediately.

The second young gorilla was curious and asked the elder chief to explain. The old gorilla told him, "The jungle looks easy but the good paths are difficult to find. Everywhere you turn, there are seemingly impenetrable thickets, loose vines and quicksand. Moreover, if you clear the jungle and reach the base of the mountain, there are many more obstacles on the way up. The mountain itself holds a grueling variety of box canyons, blind alleys, tricky ledges and loose rocks. Yet, it also offers some hidden passages and friendly caves—if you can find them."

The young gorilla was surprised. "Wow!" he exclaimed. "It all looked so simple from the village. Would you tell me about these obstacles and pathways?"

"I'll do better than that," the old gorilla replied. "I'll accompany you on your journey. You'll have to make your own way. I can't carry you or do the leg work for you—but I can guide you from time to time about direction and pace."

And so they departed, young and old together, the strong, young gorilla in search of the mountaintop and the wise old gorilla along to offer help when requested. Theirs was a difficult journey through the jungle and up the mountain. The young gorilla was amazed that the older gorilla always kept an even pace, never appeared to tire or become dejected with the many problems they encountered. In fact, he seemed able to anticipate many obstacles and avoid them.

Upon reaching the mountaintop, the young gorilla thanked the elder and asked why he had taken the time to help the young gorilla find his way. The old gorilla smiled and said, "I was once young and strong myself. Unlike your friend, I knew I wasn't invincible and, like you, I realized I could benefit from the knowledge of an experienced old gorilla that had already climbed the mountain. I was lucky enough to encounter such a gorilla—and smart enough to listen and learn. His last request was that I become elder chief and, if ever given the opportunity, return the favor of mentorship to another deserving young gorilla. You are he."

The first young gorilla was not heard from for many years. When he did return, he reported to the band that the jungle had taken its toll on him. He had made several wrong turns and was mauled constantly by the thickets. He had been hurt in falls from loose vines, lost his way many times and almost lost his life in a hidden bed of quicksand. He looked haggard but was glad to have found his way safely back home. He was surprised to learn that the other young gorilla, upon returning from the mountaintop, had been unanimously named vice chief by the elders of the band.

The moral of the story is this: On your way to the top, find an old gorilla to help you through the jungle. He knows where all the pathways are, and also the quicksand.

CHAPTER 1

IT'S A JUNGLE OUT THERE

A "rut" is merely a grave with both ends kicked out.
—Zig Ziglar

Okay, so where are you in your life and career? On track? A little confused? Indecisive? Do you feel like you are plowing through a jungle and can't see what lies ahead?

Even if you feel that you are at the top of your game, navigating the jungles of life and business is tricky business and it helps if you take an "Old Gorilla" along.

Whether in life or business, working through challenges is a process and most low achievers just don't get it. The ones I've met spend a great deal of their time complaining. They blame others for their problems and they beg random people for help in mending the consequences of their poor judgment rather than seeking informed advice on how to move forward. High achievers seem to understand there is a necessary process to pursue but many I've met were too proud, too confident or too busy (read that as "too dumb") to seek counsel about the best next steps.

High achievers are strong people and, while they make strong mistakes, they are usually strong enough to fix them satisfactorily. The problem comes from the time and energy lost in the fix that might have been avoided with a beforehand conversation. If you are a smart high-achiever who has the ability to design a great process, to accomplish wonderful things or to rally people in a grand endeavor, then there are two times in your life when you need excellent, informed advice: Now and Later.

This is where the old gorilla comes in. Successful old gorillas were once young gorillas, like you, and have either made similar mistakes or learned to avoid the mistakes waiting for them. Old gorillas have either stepped in the quicksand or have been warned about it—and know how to walk around it. They have either chosen the correct paths by the painful and time-consuming trial-and-error method or they had the benefit of guidance from their own old gorilla. They also had the good sense to listen, consider and make thoughtful choices.

I have been that old gorilla for many people in my lifetime and I have certainly benefitted from the advice of others, as well. I have done my best to record some of the most valuable of all those lessons for you in this book—things I've learned along the way and that others have found helpful in their journeys.

Read on for guidance and then seek out your old gorilla with experience in the specific type of challenge you are facing. Your old gorilla can help you set a straight path, chart your course and then adjust it when you get off track.

Most importantly, choose your old gorilla wisely, especially for specific advice on a specific issue. After all, when you take other's advice and do what they did, you have to be prepared to get what they got. If you don't like what they got—find another old gorilla.

CHAPTER 2

YOU'RE NOT AS LOST AS YOU THINK YOU ARE

Good news: *You are not special.*

That is, your troubles are likely not unique. Most everyone goes through the same life issues at one time or another. Like ships, we all go through the same channels and passages; we face the same shallows and reefs. Everybody's boat gets grounded, including yours, and some boats even get ruined on the rocks they did not see—or just didn't pay attention to. We think our problems are exceptional (and they are—to us) but they generally fall into one of these categories: money, kids, relationships, business, health or indecision.

Success is about solving problems. Some of our problems just happen—we don't create them. For example, I genetically inherited arthritis from my father and can't do anything about that. What I can do is take the advice of informed experts and people who have successfully self-treated. I can abate the issue through diet, exercise and over-the-counter medication.

I also have had problems I did create—not on purpose, of course. I either guessed wrong, didn't do my homework or just went brain dead. It happens. *Regrets are a waste of time.*[1] Just try to learn from the experience, lose the problem, keep the lesson and move on.

---

[1]   Frederico Fellini

Successful people are not people without problems. They have simply learned to deal with their problems successfully.

Your sense of problems and how critical they seem to you can have a crippling effect on your performance. But, here is what I have learned: how you think about your problems can keep them from becoming crippling. *In fact, being intentional about the way you think about a problem is the first step to solving it.* When you are confronting what are—or seem to be—critical issues, the stress created as the issues dominate your thoughts can keep you awake at night and cloud your judgment during the day. What one single action on your part can dramatically and positively impact not only your mindset but also the actual problems themselves? Here is the answer.

Write It All Down: Isolate and Conquer

> *"Circular and chaotic thinking leads to a chaotic life.*
> *Focus on a goal—any goal—and you become grounded."*
> Joe Rogers, Jr./BT

Take out a piece of paper and write down every problem you have. Do not describe the problem to yourself or record how you feel about it. Do not categorize or prioritize. Just make a list of the basic problems as quickly as they come to mind.

The problem with problems is that they seem to multiply in your head. You lie awake at night and focus on one problem. As you worry about a fix for it, another problem tries to work its way in saying, "Hey! I'm important, too. Think about me!" The mind dances from problem to problem, worrying about them all and afraid to lose the train of thought on any one of them. Eventually the initial problem works its way back in line and actually feels like a brand new problem, which it is not.

Getting all the issues on paper breaks that cycle. You will sleep better that very night knowing you have all the problems corralled, even when you do not yet have a single fix. If one of these problems pops up in your mind you can simply tell yourself, "I've got it; it's on the list. I'll think about it tomorrow."

When tomorrow does come, you have all the issues in front of you and you can think about them in an orderly way. Circle the real problems and cross out the ones that tried to look important last night but really are not. You can then prioritize your circles and decide which issues to attack first. Isolating your problems on paper gives you the room and confidence to think them through.

When you sit down with your mentor (old gorilla) and seek advice, this list will guide you both through a thoughtful process. Without the list, you will simply be a sleepless worrier.

CHAPTER 3

CHOOSING YOUR PATH

Experience is what you get right after you needed it.
—Steven Wright

Get focused. Get some direction in your life. Most ships run aground when they lose power and are pushed around by the wind and currents. Ships under power run the channels much more effectively than ships adrift.

It can be tough to establish direction and purpose in your life when life is being tough on you. "What is really important?" you ask. "Where do I start? How do I stay on track?"

If you don't know what you really want out of life or business, it is unlikely your mentor will be able to help you find it. Try these ideas to explore those important questions and arrive at thoughtful, useful answers.

What IS Really Important?

Here is a tool to organize your thoughts around your needs, your wants and the things you really dislike. It's a way to get grounded when you are trying to make decisions in the confusion of life. I call it a "personal reality check."

On a piece of blank paper, draw two vertical lines dividing the paper into three equal columns. Label the first column "Must Have." Label the second column "Like to Have" and call the third column something like "Will Not Tolerate" or "Will Not Put Up With."

Now consider your life, your family circumstances or the decision at-hand and start filling in the columns. In the first column, list all those outcomes that are absolutely essential to your life now and in the future. If considering a specific decision, also include the outcomes that you would absolutely demand happen as a product of that decision. In the second column, place all the outcomes that would be nice to see, but are not critical. These are bonus items you would like to have but really can do without. These are not deal-breakers.

The third column is a little tricky. It represents outcomes, eventualities and actions you would not tolerate in your life. For a specific decision at-hand, these are the outcomes you would not abide at the conclusion of the deal you are considering. At a glance, you might think it is the opposite of column one—and sometimes it is. Actually, it is the "I won't go there no matter what" column. The more honest you are about what you place in this column and the more you pay attention to it, the happier and less frustrated you will be.

For example:

What Is Important to Me in Life

Must Have	Like to Have	Will Not Tolerate
Health	Great paying job	Bad health habits
Fitness	New car	Job I hate
Loving spouse	Home vs. apartment	People who lie, cheat, steal

Children	Friendly in-laws	Poor schools for my children
Stable job with room to grow	A leadership role in job/community	
Good friends		
Ample money		
Savings account		
Living expenses covered		

Here is how a personal reality check diagram might work for someone considering a job change.

What I Want in a New Job

Must Have	Like to Have	Cannot Abide
At least $90k/year	> $100k/year	Move out of southeast
Good health benefits	Stock purchase opportunity	More stress than now
A leadership role	Company car	Incompetent boss
Growth opportunity	Officership opportunity	
Competent, friendly bosses and associates	Based in Florida	
Job in sales or management	Less stress than now	

Now you are grounded and ready to move forward through the jungle.

Where Do I Start?

There is an old story about the toothbrush salesman who was overwhelmed by all the people he could sell his product to. He knew everyone needed a toothbrush but could not decide where to start. The salesman's problem was solved when his sales manager told him to find a rock, throw it in the air and stand on top of the rock wherever it landed. The savvy sales manager said the next person who walked by was the salesman's first potential toothbrush customer. Problem solved.

It sounds silly but it's true. Some people are waiting for the perfect moment, the perfect situation or the perfect circumstances to get started. Here is a newsflash: all the suns and moons and planets will not line up together again in your lifetime or mine. *Bloom where you are planted.* The perfect time to start is **now** and the perfect place to start is **where you are**. By the way, it's exactly the same time and place all other successful people started.

How Do I Stay on Track?

Here is another tool to help sort that out. When making decisions, some people use a "T" chart to list the "pluses and minuses" (good and bad things) about the expected outcome of the decision. It is a good way to stay focused on the decision process. It says, "If I do this, here are the positives I expect and here are the negatives I expect. Now, what makes sense?"

The idea of a T Chart is to list the pros and cons of a particular decision on either side of the stem of a T. If there are more pros than cons, move forward. If not, don't. You can also assign each pro and con a number value based on its importance, and then go with the decision of the column with the highest value.

Should I buy a new car?

+		−	
+3	Newer car, better image	Old car runs ok (just)	(-2)
+1	Better gas mileage	New car, new car payment	(-3)
+2	More reliable	Won't get much on trade-in	(-1)
+3	I'd feel better		
+1	Less maintenance $		
+3	My budget will allow it		
(+13)	Total	Total	(-6)

Using the "T" chart tool and the reality check tool for decisions should lead you in the right direction. It will not be the perfect direction because there is no "perfect" direction in the real world.

> *"Life does not consist in holding good cards but rather in playing well the hands you are dealt."* —Jack London

Staying on track throughout the successful journey is not about perfect circumstances and perfect decisions. If it were, nobody could do it. Staying on track is about choices and consequences.

Think about your own personal journey this way. Imagine a huge compass lying on the ground and you are standing in the center looking forward at due North. The N at the top of the compass is where you want to be. The N is your goal, your vision or your personal dream. Most folks think the journey should be straight up the compass to N, but that's not the way it works in life. The trick is to make decisions that lead you basically north on the compass anywhere between due East and due West, headed toward N. It's a zigzag route. There is no perfect path. Just don't back up by making crazy choices, the consequences of which will lead you to the south side of E and W—away from your goal.

It's like stepping stones in a creek. Choose the good stones, even if they are not in a straight line, and keep moving forward toward the other bank. For each big decision (and many of the small ones) ask yourself, "If I make this choice, will it take me basically toward my goal or away from it?"

Reversible Versus Irreversible Decisions

Decisions to be made come in all sizes from small to huge and in a variety of shapes but there are really only two kinds of decisions: Reversible and Irreversible.

A reversible decision can be incorrectly made and then changed with little consequence, like buying the wrong size shirt or accidently scheduling an office meeting on a holiday date.

Don't agonize over reversible decisions. If it's not a big deal and if it was you who got it wrong, admit it, countermand (correct) the decision and move on. Nobody gets all the little decisions right. The job is to get most of them right.

Not so with irreversible decisions. These are decisions whose consequences are life and business altering for you or someone else. They either cannot be changed or changing them would be very expensive. At worst, you are unable to correct the damage that was created due to the error. The fact that a decision will be irreversible is apparent to people who take the time to carefully consider: *Who and what is impacted by this decision and to what magnitude? What are the consequences of success? What are the consequences of failure? What are the unforeseen consequences (what am I not considering)?*

Really Big Decisions

There are eight major personal, irreversible decisions that control where you (and your children) land in life.

1. It all starts with high school and what you (or your children) do after each school day is finished. (Structure counts at this age.)
   • Do you play sports, band, drama, join clubs? Or, do you hang out at the mall with friends? If you do just hang out with friends, at least hang out with friends with ambition.

2. If and where you go to college or trade school.
   • Not just what you study—rather, the contacts you make for later in life and future business relationships.

3. Where you go to work.
   • Who you work for, and where.

4. If and who you marry.
   • Is your partner your social equal? Does your partner have people skills? Share your ambition? Balance your strengths and weaknesses?

5. Where you live.
   • City, state and neighborhood.

6. Children or no children.
   • It's just a decision. You have more time early on with no kids. This can have a huge impact later with no continuing family.

7.   Whether or not you save money.
  - How do you handle your finances in general? Do you have a plan? A budget? Or do you wing it?

8.   How you relate to the world spiritually.
  - Through organized religion? Personal spirituality? Or none?

Each of these decisions will send you (or your children) down a very specific path. Think about it.

The options of any important decision will involve emotion but also the reality of social or business mathematics. *Do the math before making the decision and…if you decide to shoot yourself in the foot, don't be surprised when it hurts.*

CHAPTER 4

CHOOSING YOUR OLD GORILLA

When the pupil is ready, the master will appear.
—Blavatsky, Parchment, et al.

I know a lot of successful people. I don't know a single one who does not now have or who has never had a mentor. A mentor is someone who will help guide you through the social, political, cultural and spiritual aspects of your life and business—the jungle.

There have been several old gorillas in my life. Some of them I didn't even know, like American motivational legends Earl Nightingale and Zig Ziglar and American entrepreneur Jim Rohn. I simply read or listened to their advice and generally followed it. Some indispensable general advice comes from reading good books, listening to good CDs and paying attention to solid, smart, successful people. You'll see a lot of inferred wisdom in these pages from sage old gorillas like Mr. Rohn, Mr. Ziglar, Mr. Nightingale and others. They got it right on advice in general.

Specific advice for a specific issue is a whole different deal. In this case, it is absolutely essential to choose an informed mentor with a track record of success on your specific issue. Just because people are knowledgeable in one area doesn't mean they know "Jack" in another. Just because someone can argue effectively does not mean he or she is right. The woods are full of very presentable (even flashy) gorillas that can bellow bravely but have no credentials and no history of success to warrant your listening to a word of it. Let me repeat what I said before: *When you do what they did, be prepared to get what they got.*

One of my mentors, a personal "old" gorilla, was nearly two years younger than me, but he was plowing through the jungle ahead and pulling me along behind. He was innately savvy about business and people, and he read a great deal—particularly biographies and industry-related material. He built one of the largest 24-hour restaurant chains on the planet and I was proud to be a part of it. He was not perfect nor did he get all the decisions 100 percent right, but he was always connected, always involved, always thinking and absolutely passionate about his business. A colleague asked me one time about the key to being successful. I told him a good way to start was to hang around this man and pay attention.

Before I turned forty years old, I got the idea to interview people in their fifties and ask them what the decade of their forties looked like. I took them to lunch, individually, and asked one question, "I'm thirty-nine. What can I expect in my forties?" The information was so good and so beneficial that I have repeated the event just prior to each milestone decade.

Even if you do not take them all to lunch, you may actually have several mentors at once who play different roles in your business and personal life. For example, you might seek out a fiscally skilled mentor for your finances but consult a "fashion guru" to get your wardrobe in order.

If you work in a medium-to-large company, you may even be assigned a mentor as a part of a corporate mentor program. This is both flattering and convenient but it may not be productive. Just because someone is nice to you does not mean he or she will be a good mentor for you. Also, the fact that a person has much more "experience" than you does not qualify them as a good coach. Ten years of experience sounds impressive but what if that person never learned anything new after the first year? That means he or she has one year's experience, ten times. Not impressive.

So, how do you pick the right mentor? The truth is that your needs and where you are in life will change from year to year and sometimes month to month. In parallel, your mentors will change over time depending on your position, circumstances and requirements. What will not change are the criteria for their selection. While there are many qualities in a great mentor, the three I think most important are:

1. A solid track record of success
2. Knowledge and experience in your specific areas of interest
3. Peer respect

Here is a fact: The more respected your mentor is by his/her peers, the greater your chances of success. Don't look for flashy or super-cool. Look for demonstrated success, local knowledge and honest respect from others. Remember, if you follow in someone's footsteps, you need to be ready to go where they went. Choose wisely.

Once you have found an excellent mentor, the job has only just begun. You own the role as "mentee" and it has some important responsibilities:

- **Check-in frequency**—It's a good idea for you and your mentor to agree on regular "catch-up" meetings. Sitting down every few weeks on a routine basis keeps the direction and the relationship on track. Knowing you have an approaching meeting with your mentor will also help organize your thoughts and questions around that meeting. Occasionally, crazy things can happen between these meetings. When that occurs, remember that you are the one seeking advice. Your mentor may have taken a mind-reading course but probably flunked it and likely does not know you are struggling with an issue. Don't be afraid to call when something unusual comes up.

- **Ask thoughtful questions**—Prepare for the conversation by organizing your thoughts and questions around your goal for the meeting. Ask yourself what you really want to learn from this meeting. Is it how to handle a specific problem or person? Is it reassurance on the direction you have decided to take? Whatever the issue, prepare your questions ahead of time and be thoughtful about their importance. You are the one holding the meeting, not the other way around.

- **Be candid**—You and your mentor can waste a great deal of time if you are not honest about your interests and concerns. Your mentor wants to help you achieve <u>your</u> goals and pursue <u>your</u> dreams, not his or hers. Your mentor may help you adjust the reality of those goals and dreams from time to time but he or she must always know your honest thoughts and opinions.

- **Share what you have learned**—Over time, the information and advice you receive from your mentor will pay off in learning experiences. Be sure to share them with your mentor for two reasons: 1) the review will help you strengthen your inventory of "things that work" and 2) your mentor will appreciate hearing about positive experiences that are accruing to your success.

- **Say "Thank you!"**—Your mentor has dedicated to you, not only time, but also a great deal of thought and effort. He worries when you worry. She smiles when you are happy. Be sure to say thank you for the time, interest and emotional connection your mentor is providing. *Generally speaking, never ever pass up a chance to say thank you for a kindness, large or small, on anyone's part.*

CHAPTER 5

NAVIGATING THE PATH USING THE BASIC LAWS OF SUCCESS

More important than "doing things right" is doing the right thing.
—Peter F. Drucker

So, you intend to be successful. Do you intend to be really successful? To the extent that one day you will retire independently wealthy?

I have travelled the country asking this question in front of many groups of bright, emerging high achievers and their answer won't surprise you. One hundred percent said this: "I'm going out into the world and will do whatever it takes, and eventually I'm going to retire independently wealthy."

That is what they all say… but is that what you see when you walk downtown? Why aren't the streets filled with 65-year-old independently wealthy people? What happened?

Statistically, here is what happened. A small group, call it 5 percent, actually do retire independently wealthy; roughly 45 percent "get by." This means they don't get ahead but they don't get behind if they stick to their budget. And the rest—are broke. They all started with high ideals and were willing to work hard, but at retirement age only 5 out of 100 retire independently wealthy. And, unbelievably, right here in America—in the land of opportunity, in the richest country in the history of the world—about 50 percent leave the American workforce requiring some form of government subsistence in order to survive.

How can that be? What did the 5 get that the 50 missed? What did the 5 learn that the 50 either failed to learn or learned and ignored? The answer is…the basic laws of success.

Some of these laws are so basic there are biblical passages about them. *"As ye sow, so shall ye reap"* is as basic as it gets. But do you really know what it means? Simply put, it means you must work hard. It means that hard work is the bedrock of success. If you were building a "house of success," hard work would be the foundation.

But, we know there is more to a house than a foundation and so there is more to success than just hard work. American writer Sam Ewing once said, *"It's not just the hours you put in your work that counts, it's the work you put in the hours."* This translates to the fact that it is not only how hard you work but also HOW you work hard. If hard work is the foundation of success, how you work hard is the structure or the framing of success—and I call these techniques "success tactics"—the basic laws of success.

How nice it would be if these basic laws were written down some place so you could look at them every day and apply them to your life every day. Would doing that propel you toward becoming one of "the 5"? Could this applied knowledge push you away from being one of "the 50"?

Here is the good news. The rest of this chapter is "the list" of those success tactics—but they come with this warning: Everything on the list is easy to do. That doesn't sound like much of a warning until you hear the rest of it: Everything on this list is also easy NOT to do. [2]

I have noticed over time that the difference between either success and mediocrity or failure is rarely the act of doing the one-time huge, gargantuan tasks. It is absolutely about being willing to do, every day, the little things that are easy to do…but also easy not to do.

So, let's talk conversationally. Here's the list. This is what the 5 got and the 50 missed. *What will you do with it?*

The Success Tactics (The Basic Laws of Success)

1. **Always make notes.** Create reminders. Don't try to remember anything. If you are an "analog" person, keep a pen and paper with you always—in your pocket or purse, in your car, at your home. If you are "digital," your smartphone or tablet should always be close and ready to make notes and reminders.

    An excellent place to keep these "note-makers" handy is at your bedside. Occasionally, late at night after you have turned out the lights and said your prayers, you are rewarded with a great idea. As one of the 5, when this happens, you turn on the light, make the note and turn off the light, drifting to sleep comfortable in the knowledge that the idea will be right there for you in the morning. One of the 50 will try to remember the idea—but, usually, do not.

    Another great place to keep note-makers handy is in the bathroom. In case you haven't noticed, many of your really

---

[2]   Jim Rone said, "What is easy to do is also easy not to do" and "Success is easy but so is neglect."

terrific ideas come to you in the bathroom. Having a real-time way to save these BFOs (blinding flashes of the obvious) will pay you big dividends!

2. **Hang around the right people.** If you want to be rich, hang around rich people. If you want to be respected, hang around respectable people. If you want to be foolish, hang around fools. Fools are good at teaching you how to appear foolish and class clowns are always looking for recruits.

    Hang around people who have things you aspire to have, do things you aspire to do and hold positions you aspire to hold. Hang around these people and LISTEN.

2.5 This is actually a part of number 2, but is so important it deserves its own number. While you are hanging around the right people, **find a mentor** (see chapter 4). This is the old gorilla we talked about. Pick one out and just ask. You'll be surprised. He or she will likely be honored you asked and delighted to do it.

    This is very important! Occasionally, when you are hanging around your mentor and other "right people," these folks will do something nice for you. WRITE THANK YOU NOTES. Many women do this instinctively; most men do not. The fact is that Thank You notes set you apart. When I receive a Thank You note from someone, I immediately lift that person out of the crowd and put them in a special place. Most substantial people do the same, not only because your act of kindness and respect is impressive but also because they understand this is how we behave in a polite society.

An email or a text is not a Thank You note unless it's for a good friend, on a very informal basis, saying thank you for a minor accommodation—as in, "Hi Suzy. Thanks again for the lift to work yesterday."

A gift or a major favor done always demands and gets a written, paper-and-pen Thank You note.

Bill Todd, Professor of the Practice at Georgia Tech, teaches in his curriculum that a thank you note has three parts. The first paragraph is "what" you appreciate, like "Dear Suzanne, I want to thank you very much for taking the time to work with me on our project." The second paragraph is conversational and expresses why you appreciate it and what it means to you, such as "Your input was instrumental in the project's success and without you, we could never have achieved the A rating we received." The third paragraph should be an affirmation of the thank you and include hopeful reciprocation or well wishes, for example: "I really appreciate the time and energy you devoted to us and hope I can help you in some way in the future" or "Thanks again for your terrific mentoring and I wish you all the best in your new career."

In the big leagues, they write Thank You notes and you should never pass up the chance to pen a sincere one.

3. **Be honest.** Long term, in business and in life, you cannot be dishonest and survive. The key words here are "long term." There is a lengthy list of people who appeared eminently successful—right up until the time they checked into prison. Their "success" was short term. Understand that dishonesty may not catch up with someone today, tomorrow, this week or this year, but eventually "the truth always comes out." Honesty

is, in fact, the best policy and you must respect that fact to be successful, long term, in business and in life. The truth is that honesty is actually easier than dishonesty. Abraham Lincoln famously said, *"No man ever got lost on a straight road."*

4. **Keep a great attitude—always!** If you forget everything else in these pages, remember this: YOUR ATTITUDE IS THE SINGLE MOST OBSERVED THING ABOUT YOU! More than your flashy car, more than your fancy clothes and more than your amazing good looks—*your attitude is the single most observed thing about you.*[3]

People with great attitudes are a magnet for great experiences. People with bad attitudes are a magnet for bad experiences.

I like to tell the story about "Jim and the doctor." Jim Hosseini is a close friend and colleague of mine who is an interesting story, himself. Jim came to America from Iran speaking high-school English, received an undergraduate and a master's degree in Accounting and now occupies a very senior position with Waffle House, one of the largest 24-hour restaurant chains in the world.

Jim embodies all of the characteristics we are discussing here (which is a reason he is so successful, one might think). We were talking one day about the importance of attitude and he told me a story about when he got up one morning with the flu. Jim called his doctor's office, made an appointment and, on arrival, used his last ounce of strength to open the office door. The receptionist looked up and said, "Good morning, Jim. How are you?" Jim told me he replied, "Great!" I asked him why he

---

[3]   From the philosophy of Jim Hosseini

said that and he responded, "Well, Bert—the fact was that everything else in my life was great. I just had the flu, which would pass. There was nothing she could do about it—so why should I ruin her day?"

Jim sat down in the office and pretty soon the nurse opened the door to take him back and said, "Good morning, Jim! How are you?" Again, Jim said, "Great!" He reminded me that she couldn't help, either. She asked the "social question" and Jim gave her the "social answer." So the nurse took Jim back to an examination room to wait for the doctor.

A short time later the door opened and the doctor entered, looked at my friend and asked, "Good morning, Jim. How are you?" Jim said, "I feel like Hell." He'd finally reached the guy who could do something about it.

Remember: Keep a great attitude <u>always</u>. It is the single most observed thing about you.

5. **Get up earlier than your friends.** If you are in business, get up earlier than your competitors. You may think that early rising is a pain in the neck or you may even have a lower opinion of it. The fact is, getting up early is simply a habit that is easy to get accustomed to. Unfortunately, so is sleeping in and, all other things equal, first one up wins. If this were true there would be an age-old proverb about it—and there is: *The early bird gets the worm.* The good news is that you don't have to be the first one up. You just have to get up before everyone else you want to beat.

6. **Learn to say yes (and) learn HOW to say NO!** But don't ever, ever say something like, "Okay, I'll do it...but I really don't

want to." When you say that, you make two people unhappy. You're unhappy because you are doing something you do not want to do and the other person is unhappy because they think you're not going to do a good job.

Sometimes people say "Yes" because they don't know how to say "No." They think it's not okay to say "No." Women in the workplace tell me they are particularly stricken with this because they think their male counterparts are all saying "Yes" (and the dumb ones probably are). "No" is a perfectly appropriate answer when someone randomly asks you to take on a task you either clearly should not be doing, don't want to do or simply don't have time for. The trick is to say it with a great deal of charm. Your response when asked to do something along those lines should sound like this: *"No, I'd love to help you out but I can't. There is something else I have to do that will keep me from doing that but I hope you find somebody else, real soon."* Say it with a smile and a great deal of charm and let the words roll right off your tongue. Once finished, shut up. The next one who talks, loses, and if you say your piece and keep quiet, expect to hear something like, "Oh, okay. Thanks anyway."

Stand in front of a mirror, relax and practice saying "NO" until it flows like water. Chances are good you'll have an opportunity to use it tomorrow. Of course, if the request comes from your thoughtful and very competent boss, the correct answer is, "I can't think of anything else I'd rather do!" Then figure out how to get it done.

7. **Nourish yourself.** There are three things you can nourish: Mind, body and soul or spirit.

For the mind: **Read**. You must read something—anything— every day. If you read something every day and I read nothing... over twenty years, all other things being equal, you will know a lot more than I do. *Never underestimate the tremendous power of small things repeated frequently over a long period of time.*

Biographer Andy Kilpatrick quotes Charlie Munger, Warren Buffet's vice-chair, as saying, "In my whole life, I have known no wise people...who didn't read all the time—none, zero."

Also for the mind: **Listen**. Realize that you have two ears and one mouth for a very good reason. Listen twice as much as you talk. When you talk you are saying something you already know; when you listen, you have the chance to learn something.

For the body: **You must eat something for breakfast every morning**. There is a physiological reason why you need to get something in your stomach within ninety minutes after getting up. The body is like a car with one key difference: there is no gas tank. The stomach is not a gas tank. It's a processing unit like the carburetor. If a car runs out of fuel, it dies. By the same principal, if the body runs out of fuel, it can also die. But your body has a failsafe system to protect you and it looks like this: If you don't eat breakfast or get something in your stomach within ninety minutes after you get up, about ten-thirty or eleven o'clock in the morning, the body sends a message to the mind. It says, "Hey, this fool didn't eat breakfast!" The mind sends a message back to the body to move to Plan B, which means that the body starts infusing directly into the blood stream an alternative emergency fuel: adrenaline. But there's a problem with this fuel; it is not the regular stuff. This is like a high octane jet fuel, which is why sometimes by eleven in the morning when you haven't eaten breakfast you get a little jittery—and those several cups of coffee you had are probably piling on. And then what happens when you go sailing right on through the morning and forget to eat lunch? (Unfortunately, we have all done it.)

Sometime, about two in the afternoon, the body sends a message to the mind again. It says, "Hey this fool is trying to kill us; he didn't eat lunch either!" The mind says, "Go to Plan C" and the body starts stripping fat and light muscle fiber from the upper arms and the upper legs. The body is literally eating itself in order to survive. Ask your doctor friends about this.

There is a medical term for this phenomenon—this infusion of adrenaline and self-consumption in order to maintain preservation. Your body has just defensively entered a mild form of *shock*.

Question: How could a leader in shock make decisions in the best interest of his or her people? How can she or he lead any number of people in any grand endeavor? Answer: You can't do it very well. And what does it take to shut that failsafe process down? Within ninety minutes after you get up, eat a piece of fruit, a slice of toast, a bowl of cereal, a full breakfast. Anything in your stomach within ninety minutes after you get up will shut that emergency process down and start you on a normal day.

Lastly, to nourish the spirit: **Pray.** Let me hasten to say that this is not a religious issue but, unless you have not noticed, you and I are not in charge. We are not even trusted with the really important stuff. Consider this: when was the last time you told your heart to beat? Do you tell yourself to breathe? How about that cut you had on your knee? Did you command it to heal so you wouldn't bleed to death? There truly is a greater force at work in this world than you and me and it is called by so many names—God, Jesus, Rahman, Allah, Mohammed, Buddha—but every culture in the world recognizes that we are not in charge, that this larger force is in control.

With this in mind, it would be nice, and it would be appropriate, if after you turn out the light at night, you would take just a minute to be grateful for the good things happening to you and ask for help with the other stuff. Can you remember ever going to bed one night with a problem heavy on your heart, and no solution in sight? You went to sleep and, somewhere in the middle of the night, the solution came to you. You woke up the next morning, had the answer and you still don't know where it came from. You are not the only one who has experienced this. Help is available if you ask for it.

8. **Learn to manage your time.** We all get the same amount of time—twenty-four hours in a day, seven days a week, 365 days a year. So why do some people accomplish more than others? The answer is they have learned how to manage their time more effectively. Here are three skills you must learn in order to manage your time more effectively:

    a. Know where you want to go—you must have goals. If you don't have your goals physically recorded somewhere—on your smartphone or computer, on a piece of paper in your pocket or purse, some place—then I can probably guess your bank balance to within a few hundred dollars. And, it will always be that way. Goals define your purpose in life. Without goals you are a wandering generality. Goals turn you into a meaningful specific.[4]

Here is an example:

If I handed you a basketball at half court and gave you ten chances to make one lay up—could you do it? "No problem," you say. But then, I blindfold you and turn you around a few times. Could you do it now? "No fair, you cry! How can I hit a goal I can't see?" That's a good question. Here is another one: *How can you achieve a goal you have not set?* Goals focus you and define your purpose in life.

If you remember the book *Alice In Wonderland*[5], Alice fell through the looking glass and encountered the nasty Queen of Hearts. While trying to get home, she came to a fork in the road, sat down and started crying. The Cheshire cat sitting in the gingham tree next to the fork in the road asked Alice why she was crying, and she said, "I don't know which road to take." The cat asked, "Where do you want to go?" Alice responded, "I don't know." And then the cat said, "Then any road will do."

If you have never set goals, you may not know how. Go back and reread the section about choosing your

---

[4]   Most of the examples of goal setting come from media developed by Jim Rone and Zig Ziglar. Mr. Ziglar coined the phrases "wandering generality" and "meaningful specific." He also suggested that, without goals, your bank balance could be roughly predicted.

[5]   An approximation of quotes from Lewis Carroll and *Alice's Adventures in Wonderland*

path and determining what really is important to you. A goal is a physical item or a personal achievement which, when attained or accomplished, will move you closer to those values, positions or holdings that are really important to your life. The most important goals are the ones that can have the greatest impact on you and your successful life. Goals are essential. They focus you, center you and define your purpose in life. You have to know where you want to go.

b. To achieve your goals, you must have an action plan. Incredibly, some people spend more time planning a party than a life. Consider your goals, marshal the resources, set deadlines and live by them. Deadlines let you know how much time is left on the clock and create a sense of urgency. A good trick to organize your time around your goals is to create a "100 Day Plan." This is the list of five or six highly impactful action initiatives that you commit to complete by a firm date 100 days from today. Work that plan every day, avoid distractions, and you will reach your goal—on time.

c. Finally, learn how to avoid distractions. There are about a thousand distractions a minute in the world, but you have to press through them and stay the course.

Think of it this way: Are you a "seed sower" or a "bird chaser"? Back in biblical times (see Matthew 13:1-23) the survival of the village depended upon the skill and perseverance of the seed sower. So, imagine you are that seed sower and you are out in the village fields.

It is a beautiful spring morning, right at dawn with a light breeze, and you have a cloth sack of seeds over your shoulder. You are walking along, throwing seeds out and everything is great... for about ten minutes. You look back and there are birds pecking at the seeds. Now, at this particular moment in your life, you have one decision to make: Do you want to be a seed sower or a bird chaser?

The seed sower knows some of those seeds he is throwing out will land on barren ground and are not going to grow. Some of them will blow up on rocks and are not going to grow and some of the seeds the birds will eat. But the seed sower knows that most of those seeds thrown out will get down into the ground, germinate and grow the crops that the village needs. The skillful seed sower also knows that, at the end of the day, 100 percent of the seeds left in that sack are definitely <u>not</u> going to grow.

Better to be a seed sower than a bird chaser. Better to stay the course and ignore the distractions. Seed sowers create value. Bird chasers tend to "major in minor affairs" and lose sight of the real goal line and time line. Bird chasers are not known for great achievements and seldom even catch birds.

9. **Give away all the credit and take all the blame.** People who do this are called leaders; people who do not are called followers. Eventually, everyone figures out who really was responsible for success and who was responsible for failure. Let them discover the facts on their own. If you "toot your own horn," it diminishes

your success. If you shirk the blame that is rightfully yours, people see you as a minor leaguer who can't take criticism.

Consider the words of legendary football coach, Paul (Bear) Bryant: *"If anything goes bad, **I did it**. If anything goes semi–good, then **we did it**. If anything goes real good, then **you did it**. That's all it takes to get people to win football games for you."*

Self-promotion is a product of personal insecurity and is as transparent as excuse making. Men and women who lead successfully don't engage in either weakness. That is just the way it works in the big leagues.

10. Here is the most powerful of the basic laws: **Give away anonymously things of value.** (Anonymously means you don't talk about it.)

I know a family who, on the first freezing day of every winter, call all the elementary schools in the community and ask one question: "Who are the children that came to school today with no coats?" Think about it—If it is 32 degrees outside and a child comes to school with no coat, there is only one reason: the child doesn't have a coat.

So, the family gets these children's genders and sizes. They go to Wal-Mart, Kmart and Burlington and they buy these kids jackets. They take them home and pin a child's information in each jacket. They put these coats into big black plastic lawn bags and the next day they take them to the school. Without giving their names, the family leaves the coats at the front desk and asks that they be given to the principal. Then they leave.

Walking down the stairs after they have done that, knowing what they have done for those children and not seeking credit for their kindness—knowing in their hearts the gift is their secret—what kind of positive power follows them all that day? And, if these anonymous acts of selfless kindness are frequent, imagine the positive power in their lives.

Certainly, there are other laws of success but these ten are the most basic. Numbers 1-9 will organize you and Number 10 will give you power you never dreamed of.

All are easy to do—and just as easy not to do.

Here is some wonderful news. You don't have to do everything discussed in this chapter. You don't even have to do any of it very well. The first few fumbling, bumbling efforts at anything you've just read will give you amazing and dramatic results. You owe it to yourself to give it a try.

CHAPTER 6

WHAT YOUR MENTOR WILL TELL YOU ABOUT LEADERSHIP—THE BAREBONES VERSION

Lead is not the same as manage and manage is not the same as facilitate.
—Joe Rogers, Jr.

For hundreds of years, in times of trouble, people desperately await the man or woman who will ride up on a white horse and tell them what to do. These saviors are called *leaders*.

Sometimes people are leaders by personal decision and sometimes they become leaders by default. But, since the beginning of time, whenever there are two or more people (or animals) gathered together, one of them will emerge as the leader.

The problems leaders face can be very complex, but the basic leadership function is not. Successful leadership is the result of an applied focus of some fairly simple but critically important fundamentals. While it is true that some of these fundamental behaviors appear to come naturally to great leaders, the fact is that excellent leadership is really an acquired skill born of personal discipline and commitment, over time.

Leadership is all about inspiring others and managing the process as they work toward great achievement. A "sprint, drift and react" approach will not work, long term. You must have a plan and a thoughtful process for its execution.

Good leadership is not only about the plan you drive but also about the behavior you do not allow. Your attentive leadership can produce tremendous results in a positive direction and those results may be derailed by inattention to the negative forces you ignore or allow. For an organization in which anything goes, eventually everything goes. Leaders not only lead, they don't let their people get lost.

The information in this chapter is not intended to be a "how to" set of instructions on leadership. What follows is a basic outline of the discussion you and your mentor should have about leadership and its fundamental elements, its critical pieces and a few editorial comments I've heard for years about the leadership model. Please review this chapter with your mentor and ask his or her opinion regarding the model itself, its components and the personal leadership characteristics listed for various leadership styles and abilities.

The Leadership Model

On what does a successful leader focus? What occupies his or her time and energy?

Here are some critically important, fundamental, strategic priorities that should command the attention of every effective leader:

- **A Focus on People**

  Recruiting (for quality and experience)
  Training (for the task)
  Developing (to the individual's full potential)
  Retaining (change saps momentum)

  Advice: Nothing in business (or life) is more important than the people with whom you surround yourself. Good people, well trained and directed to your mission, can bring terrific results. Mediocre people, or good people who are frustrated with poor training and direction, will produce lackluster to poor results while eating up capital and assets.

- **Effective Planning**

   Mission (clearly defined)
   Strategy (the overall plan to achieve success)
   Tactics (directing the team effort day to day based on evolving events)

   Advice: Be careful about creating "inspirational" mission statements and emotionally charged strategic or tactical plan announcements that are designed to "fire up the team" but are devoid of specifics. The battle cry, "Be all you can be!" sounds exciting but it means a thousand things to a thousand different people. If you really want achievement, spell out exactly where the goal line is. For example: "Close the deal by 5 p.m. on Friday and stay within my previously stated guidelines. Call me when it's done but don't call me any later than 5:15." This direction leaves little room for personal interpretation.

- **Efficient Execution**

   Show up (99 percent of business success is about the leader showing up personally and executing)
   Direct (first be effective, then be efficient)
   Evaluate (you can't manage what you don't measure)
   Redirect (have specific instructions for someone falling short of your expectations)

Advice: There are some things you just can't "phone in" and real-time direction in the execution phase of a project leads the list. I'm not telling you to micro-manage. What I am saying is that your physical or verbal presence in the middle of the action lends strength to the cause and brings focus to the direction. My business adaptation on Newton's First Law in physics is this: "People and objects in motion tend to remain in motion and people and objects at rest tend to remain at rest until acted upon by an outside force." You, of course, are that force! Sometimes you can actually have impact by showing up and saying nothing. Consider this other loosely interpreted law of physics: "A force moving through a field tends to organize the field simply by its presence." To illustrate this, recall your grade school science experiment: a clump of metal filings sits randomly on a piece of paper until the magnet is passed underneath the paper. Without touching the field of filings, the magnetic force picks them up, organizes them and lays them back down in perfect order as it passes by. Sometimes, the silent power of your respected leadership presence will tend to organize the effort and pick up the pace.

- **Crisis Management—Embrace It and Attack It**

If you are a leader, you absolutely <u>will</u> experience a crisis. In fact, you will experience many of them. It comes with the territory. In a crisis, the team's rank and file will tend to go into an emotional stampede. Your job as the leader is to be the voice of reason in chaos. Reflect on your past experiences and think about the truth of this statement: Six months after a crisis, very few people remember the crisis but everyone remembers the attitude of the leader during the crisis. Napoleon once said, "My best generals are not those who make great decisions in peace but those who make good decisions in the crisis of war."

Advice: In a crisis, take a deep breath, thoughtfully consider your options and start giving orders. The first action order is the most important; not so much for what it says but that it is being given and that it begins to move people from a state of paralysis into corrective action. Subsequent orders become easier as the effort is energized and takes direction. Immediate, solid decisions and direction on your part, even if they seem unspectacular at the time, will accrue to your excellent leadership reputation. Indecision and silence will sink you.

- **Personal, Ongoing Self-development**

   Your self-development plan should call for a mature, applied focus over many years. At its best, your self-development is a never-ending process of discovery and construction. Roger Turner, a friend and very successful Waffle House operator was always quick to caution, "Just when you think you're a star, the wheels fall off!" What he meant was that the leadership function is a fluid, dynamic, evolving thing and you had better match the pace. The leader who thinks he or she is at the pinnacle of personal development is naïve, at best, and delusional, at worst. If your company or your position of responsibility is growing faster than you are, be prepared to fall behind.

   Advice: It takes courage to grow, especially after you're grown. Keep learning. If you don't know, you don't grow.

So, within the model, how does leadership work? Let's dig a little deeper into the action steps.

Here is what a leader is required to do:

1. Create the vision.

2. Design the mission.
3. Marshal the necessary resources.
4. Direct the execution process.
5. Measure the results.
6. Follow-up, follow-up and follow-up endlessly.
7. Redirect, cheer, thank, inspire and issue consequences—good and bad.

Vision—Great leaders have great vision. Specifically, the "mind's eye" of a great leader will form a very vivid picture of the goal at hand and begin to explore paths to progress in the achievement of that goal. The paths may change based on the leader's evaluation of what is and is not working, but the vision remains crystal clear. This is what drives the leader unswervingly toward the goal—and the more vivid the vision, the greater the chances for success.

I have known leaders who told me they put the vision on paper. I think what they meant is they wrote down the goal or the plan to achieve it. A leader's vision is a living thing that cannot be captured on paper. The leader is always communicating with the vision and the vision talks back. This may sound strange but, as a leader, it has to happen to you just once in order to realize what a powerful force this is.

Mission—To say a leader must design the mission would be trite. If not the leader, then who?

While an efficient leader may ask others to work out the day-to-day, operational tactics of a mission, the basic overall strategy—what some people would call "The Big Picture"—belongs to the leader. An example of the difference between tactics and strategy is that "tactical" is the act of driving the troops on the ground. "Strategic" is pulling up to 10,000 feet in altitude to see if the bridge is out ahead of you.

The "mission" is really the design of a comprehensive plan to achieve the goal; completely addressing all the FAQs: "Who, What, When, Where, Why and How."

Marshaling Resources—There is no substitute in business for a strong bench (good people in reserve), experience, good leadership and cash. The mission will require many resources and it is the leader's job to acquire them or ensure they are acquired. These resources may include people, capital, assets, ideas or any number of other necessities, but the leader will make sure they are all on hand for the mission and will not allow time and energy wasted in the pursuit of non-mission-essential resources or resources that can even be counterproductive to the mission. Delegates can get lost in this maze. The diligent leader with a clear vision will not.

The most important resource a leader must acquire is a cadre of excellent people, the most critical asset. Experience in these people is helpful but raw skills are essential. Be sure to look for "people-bility" (the ability to coordinate successfully with a variety of personalities in a positive way), a "get-it-done attitude" (in a battle, you want people who are looking for bullets, not stretchers) and "smarts." You can't teach any of these characteristics but if you find someone who exemplifies all three, you can teach them your business and they will surprise you with their adaptivity and results.

Texas businessman Greg Hulett always stresses the importance of acquiring the exceptional men and women who are "solution providers" rather than the "problem identifiers" who come a dime a dozen. One more thing: As you develop your team and move players into more responsible positions, you will constantly be faced with the decision of choosing between the steady "can-do" person versus the steely eyed "want-to" up-and-comer. When change is necessary, don't be afraid to take "want to" over "can do" and go early with rising talent.

Execution—*Execution wins out over brilliance!*

The plan is in place. The mission is set. The team and its resources are assembled. And all of this goes nowhere until the leader begins directing his or her people in the execution process. This direction entails three critical features:

1. Give clear and specific WRITTEN instructions.
2. Ask, "Do you know what I want? Do you have what you need?"
3. Make the deadlines for completion absolutely clear. An assignment without a deadline for completion and consequences for the outcome is just a suggestion. Leaders lead. They don't suggest.

As you work hard and execute you may become frustrated with the process. A good rule of thumb to remember is this: *If you begin to feel overwhelmed, you probably are not delegating enough.*

Measuring Results—As the execution of the plan gathers speed, we experience some early success… or do we? The diligent leader is always measuring results because he or she knows *you cannot manage what you do not measure.*[6] The mind's eye works well on visual concepts but nothing, repeat, nothing, takes the place of an accurate spreadsheet and a good database to keep the effort on track. Evaluate, but don't be so obsessive about it that it bogs you down. *Paralysis by analysis*[7] is a very common business disease.

Following Up, Redirection, Inspiration: AKA The Rest of the Story—The bulk of the leader's load until successful achievement of the goal becomes a continuing cycle of evaluation through data

---

[6]   Peter F. Drucker said, "If you can't measure it, you can't manage it."

[7]   Paralysis by analysis is a concept discussed by Harold S. Geneen and Arthur Ashe, among others.

examination, personal on-site follow up and the act of cheering and thanking success while admonishing and redirecting failure.

Admonishment, by the way, does not have to be all that painful. Everybody makes mistakes and, when I was the one in the hot seat, the best leaders I have worked for would explain where I screwed up and move immediately to a dialogue about the fix. Once assured I was back on track, the conversation was about expectations, timing and success, not about blame and guilt. As Blanchard and Johnson noted in their classic *The One-Minute Manager*, people who feel good about themselves produce good results.

Consequences are absolutely critical to direction—as critical as a steering wheel is to an automobile. Good performance gets good consequences. But, if the performance is bad, it is important that the consequence reflects both the magnitude of and the responsibility for the failure. In a great leader's organization these consequences are pre-signaled, well understood and are never a surprise.

Leadership endures problem after problem and crisis after crisis. At times, as the person in charge, it feels as if you are working on nothing but fires around your feet. The skillful leader will address these urgent (and often not relatively important) problems but never to the exclusion of the mainstream mission, which is set apart and measured daily on its own for progress.

The truly great leader has one more essential characteristic: *perseverance.* This strength is not found in managers who succumb to the inevitable problems of life and business. The concept cannot be described any more emphatically than by these two iconic world leaders:

> *Nothing in the world can take the place of*
> *persistence. Talent will not; nothing is more*
> *common than unsuccessful men with talent.*

Genius will not; unrewarded genius is almost a proverb. Education will not; the world is full of educated derelicts. Persistence and determination alone are omnipotent. The slogan "PRESS ON" has solved and always will solve the problems of the human race.
—Calvin Coolidge

"Never, never, never give up. If you are going through Hell, keep going."
—Winston Churchill

The last message on the leadership role is this: The leader's job is to ignore personal preferences (including his or her own) and find out what works.

Leaders always find a way to succeed.[8]

Strong and Weak Leaders

If you ever find yourself in charge of a "salvage" operation; that is, your task is to clean up another leader's mess, pray that he or she was a weak leader. Weak leaders make weak mistakes and they are usually fairly easy to fix. Strong leaders make strong mistakes but fortunately they are generally strong enough to correct those mistakes. If you have to come in behind a strong leader who screwed up and left, bring your lunch. You are going to be there for a while and you definitely will have your work cut out for you.

It is important to note that, leadership-wise, weak does not always equal bad and strong does not always equal good. What really defines a "good" leader is that leader's consistent track record of success in achievement for his or her projects and his or her people. If you want

---

[8]   This quote is from Michael Jordan (and others, in various forms).

to become that good leader, strong leader, successful leader, there are some truths you need to embrace:

First, before you can lead, it is important to understand that 50 percent of the leadership you get paid to provide is to yourself. Businesses and people get lost when their leaders get lost.

Additionally, there are some basic skills and characteristics requisite to excellent, effective leadership and it is important that you both understand and appreciate them. If you do not now personally possess these skills and characteristics, I encourage you to work on acquiring them. Strength in theses areas always seems to produce savvy, well-rounded, well-respected leaders.

Basic Leadership Skills—The Good Ones

A successful leader must be competent at four things:

- Understanding concepts and ideas
- Understanding, managing and developing people
- Understanding financial matters, both business and personal
- Understanding self-discipline, self-respect, self-confidence and self-image

The truly successful leader is the voice of reason in conflict. He or she exhibits depth of thought, strong core values, moral fiber and is willing to take full responsibility for all of life and business. He/she dresses, acts and talks like a professional.

The successful leader is also very adept at brokering relationships, both internally (between people within the entity he or she leads) and externally (between that entity and the organizations and leaders with which it makes contact).

Basic Leadership Fails—Not So Good

Conversely, the unsuccessful (or soon-to-be unsuccessful) leader takes "shallow cuts," giving and taking convenient answers while blaming the world for his or her problems.

At the bottom of the leadership food chain, you will find failed (or failing) leaders who show one or more of these fatal flaws:

- Self promotion (It's all about me)
- Arrogance (You and your ideas don't count)
- Abrasive style (My way or the highway)
- Sloppiness (Behavior, dress, planning, analysis)
- Naivety (But he said he would…)
- Dishonesty (Thou shalt not…)
- Uncontrollably bad temper (This is the greatest employee turnover generator)
- Insecurity (What can I do to make you love me?)
- Immaturity (Can you believe the way he acted? How embarrassing!)
- Poor grammar (A great distraction to effective communication)
- Inability to handle money (If you can't handle your money, why should I let you get close to mine?)

Possessing a few of these leadership flaws leads to a slow demise. Even more makes for a quick leadership death.

In 2008, Don Keuogh, president of The Coca-Cola Company from 1981 to 1993 and a director at Warren Buffet's company, Berkshire Hathaway, released a book entitled *The Ten Commandments of Business Failure*. This observation was based upon his lifetime in business. The ten things he lays out for guaranteed failure are:

1. Quit taking risks.
2. Be inflexible.
3. Isolate yourself.
4. Assume infallibility.
5. Play the game close to the foul line.
6. Don't take time to think.
7. Put all your faith in experts and outside consultants.
8. Love your bureaucracy.
9. Send mixed messages.
10. Be afraid of the future.

And finally, **Six Truths About Leadership**…

As a young leader in the emerging Waffle House organization, I emphasized what I called The Six Truths About Leadership:

1. You own your organization and all of its people, problems and opportunities. Period.
2. No one else is responsible for your organization. What happens or fails to happen depends strictly upon your action or your inaction.
3. What drives your people is your own force of personality and their belief in you.
4. What creates impact is your awareness, your clear and specific direction, your deadlines and your follow up.
5. An organization without discipline will self-destruct over time and take you with it.
6. You are not the faultfinder. You are the leader, the image, the vision, the plan, the execution and the energy level of your organization.

At the time, I thought I was talking about restaurant leadership. Forty years later, I realize these truths are universal in business.

EPILOGUE

It was never the intention of this book to be the end-all/be-all answer to life's problems and solutions. It was simply a hopeful effort to help you lift yourself out of the fog and lead you to the doorstep of the best, most effective mentor for you at this particular time in your life.

Are you ready to navigate the jungle? Here are some of the key points I've made for reference during your journey:

- **Seek a mentor:** As you travel through the jungle of life, it helps if you take an "Old Gorilla" along. He or she knows where all the pathways are, and also the quicksand. Look for someone with experience in your specific area of concern—someone who is respected by his or her peers. *Remember: If you do what they did, you have to be willing to get what they got.*

- **Learn from your mistakes:** When you mess up and make a bad decision, try to learn from the experience, lose the problem, keep the lesson and move on. Regret is a waste of time.

- **Be intentional:** The way you think about a problem can be the first step to solving it. Capture all the problems swimming around in your head by recording them on paper. Sleep on it, and then come back to identify and prioritize the real problems so you can think them through. When considering a change, do the homework. Don't just take the next bus painted a different color.

- **Do a personal reality check:** To get some direction in your life, start by identifying your needs, wants and dislikes. What are your deal-breakers? What will you not tolerate? What irreversible decisions have already been made? (See the "Really Big" eight decisions that determine where you may land.)

- **Chart your course and stay on track:** Use the "T" chart to diagram pros and cons on a decision to keep you moving in the right direction. There is no perfect path; just make sure you continue heading north toward your goal.

- **Follow the Basic Laws of Success:** If you want to be really successful, re-read and earnestly follow the "Success Tactics" in Chapter 5 (all easy to do but also easy not to do). From small but important habits (like writing Thank You notes) to big and important habits (like nourishing your body, mind and spirit; learning to say NO; and giving anonymously things of value), following these basic laws of success really will lead you along the right path. And, remember, keep a great attitude—always!

- **Review the Leadership Model:** Focus on your people, effective planning, efficient execution, crisis management and ongoing self-development to create the whole leadership package. Discuss the components of leadership with your mentor to apply these ideas to your specific role and learn how to avoid the pitfalls of failed (or failing) leaders.

Finally, we have talked about the two challenges you will continue to face throughout your life: problem-solving and opportunity maximization. Hopefully, the smart application of these ideas will lead you to great success.

Realize that as you learn, evolve and grow personally, change will be required and sometimes this change can be painful. During those times it is important to remember this: *Pain is inevitable but suffering is optional.*[9]

---

[9]   Dan Mager paraphrasing the heralded author and philosopher, Victor Frankl

As you go through this process, understand there are always seven steps involved in any kind of change.

1. Denial that change is needed
2. Awareness/acceptance that change is needed
3. The decision to change
4. The attempt to change
5. Failure
6. Re-engagement and perseverance
7. Successful change

You can realize wonderful and effective change, if you don't get hung up on number 5.

Happy travels!

Bert

WHAT I LEARNED ALONG THE WAY

I haven't had that many original thoughts in my life. Most of my success has come from being a good student of thoughtful, successful people. I would watch them and do what they did; listen to them and try what they said.

When you think about it, there really is not much new going on these days—just a different crowd doing it. But, occasionally, we get lucky enough to encounter a unique individual who surprisingly acts in an impressive way that gets our attention: someone who says the often-said thing in a different way that makes perfect sense to us. This presents a wonderful opportunity to learn, if we pay attention.

This book was a conundrum for me because so much of my life has been spent absorbing the great ideas and words of wisdom I've read or heard—to the extent that, at this moment in my life, I honestly don't recall all the sources of all that wisdom, much of which appears throughout the pages of this book.

What I can tell you is that these are probably not my bright ideas or clever comments. In the footnotes and acknowledgements, I've tried to list the real masters of these words and phrases that have made sense to me and positively impacted my life. Understanding that, and with humble apologies to anyone left out unintentionally, here are some guiding thoughts worth your consideration in the areas of business and personal success. Some are cute, all are thoughtful and each one is sage advice for the steady traveler on the road to success—which is always under construction.

10 Guiding Thoughts for Business Success

1. Knowing is not doing. Talk is not work. Information is not execution.
2. Learn to spot passionate and responsible but truly misinformed decisions.
3. Don't dilute a great idea with the compulsion to make a long list.
4. Old people, new problems—okay. New people, old problems—okay. Old people, old problems—not okay.
5. Talk more about ideas, less about things and not at all about people, except to evaluate them.
6. Give direct answers and don't hedge. You'll be respected if you do this and thought incompetent if you don't.
7. Being able to balance your life has more to do with you than with your business.
8. You may not have control but you can certainly have influence.
9. Don't be the person who blindly charges along with all the confidence of a fast dog staked on a slack chain.
10. Vacations are like restrooms. The closer you get to one, the more you need it.

10 Guiding Thoughts for Personal Success

1. You cannot chase success and happiness. We attract it by the person we become.[10]
2. A key component to success is with who you are in a business or a personal relationship.
3. Tell me and I'll hear. Show me and I'll see. Get me involved and I'll understand.[11]
4. Add value before you expect reward.
5. When you get angry, it's never for the reason you think you're angry. Think about it.
6. Sometimes winning the argument is not worth losing the relationship.
7. Be aware that emotional cycles are inevitable—for you and for everyone else.
8. You try a lot of things in life. Some of them work. Some don't. Learn to live with it.
9. Things are never as good or bad as they seem.
10. If you wait until all the lights are green before you leave the house, you'll never get to the grocery store.

---

[10] Jim Rohn—"Success is not to be pursued; it is to be attracted by the person we become."

[11] Approximation of the similar Chinese proverb

10 Guiding Thoughts for Leadership Success

1. Systems rule. No systems means no sustainability.
2. Don't be distracted by the wave action above the depths of the ocean.
3. When reality conflicts with theory, go with reality.
4. If it ain't broke, don't fix it.[12]
5. Your moments are other people's memories.
6. Never try to teach a pig to sing. It wastes your time and annoys the pig.[13]
7. You'll never get 100 percent of the information you need to make a decision. Just make it and get used to the stress.
8. Everything is negotiable.[14]
9. When you speed up the train, expect a few of the back cars to fall off.
10. Only a fool takes for himself the respect that is given his office. —Aesop

---

[12] T. Bert Lance, among others

[13] Robert Heinlein

[14] This quote is widely used. Carrie Fisher famously added, "Whether or not the negotiation is easy is another thing."

10 Guiding Thoughts for Any Path To Success

1. The average person gets frustrated when he can't see input and output, cause and effect, or effort and results at the same time. The scales don't balance every day. If you expect it, also expect to be frustrated.
2. Fashionable form attracts a single digit percentage of the population. Substance attracts the rest.
3. You can't learn anything until you're ready.[15]
4. History really is the great teacher. Other people's experience is a better teacher if the result is bad.[16]
5. After the heat dies down, be sure you are married to your best friend.
6. Mediocrity requires aloofness and arrogance to maintain its dignity.[17]
7. Everything has a limit. Trees don't grow to the sky.
8. There is a butt for every seat. You build the seat and someone will come along and sit down in it.
9. Any problem you can fix with money is not a real problem... even if you don't have the money.
10. If you were on your deathbed and someone asked, "What do you regret not doing?" Whatever your answer, start on that—now.[18]

I don't think a person can get enough of these motivating, commonsense ideas. They become "BFOs" (Blinding Flashes of the Obvious) and they

---

[15] John Veitch, among others

[16] Romanian proverb: "Only the foolish learn from their experience. The wise learn from other's experience."

[17] Approximation of a quote by Charles G. Dawes

[18] From the thoughts of Ramon Nuez

spark other positive ideas in our heads. I try to find and read BFOs every chance I get.

When challenged with the notion that "motivation doesn't last long," Zig Ziglar responded, "Well, neither does bathing. That's why we recommend it daily."

ACKNOWLEDGEMENTS

My "I am grateful for…" list is too long to publish here. These are some of the many people who have positively impacted my life by thought, word or deed and whose written or spoken thoughts I have shared with you in this effort.

If you get the chance to talk with, listen to or review the works of these folks, it will accrue to your success.

- Jim Rohn—American Entrepreneur, author and motivational speaker
- Earl Nightingale—The "Father of Motivational Speakers"
- Zig Ziglar—Philosopher, author and motivational speaker
- Peter F. Drucker—The "father of modern business management"
- Albert Thornton, Sr.—The fellow I was talking about when I said, "My daddy used to tell me…"
- Aspen, Chaice and Mayson—my daughters who brought the millennial perspective
- Joe W. Rogers, Jr.—Chairman and builder of Waffle House
- Joe W. Rogers, Sr.—Co-founder of Waffle House
- Jim Hosseini—Senior leader at Waffle House and common sense philosopher
- Judy Thomas Blanton—Restaurant entrepreneur
- Bob Bowman—Keeper of the "Book of Phrases Heard"
- Katherine Kelbaugh—Founding Principal of The Museum School of Avondale Estates
- Andrew Kilpatrick—Author of Warren Buffet's biography, *Of Permanent Value*
- Mike Smith—who brought the engineer's perspective

- Sabina Vajraca—who brought the artist and film director's perspective
- Alex Abney—my college-aged friend who is wise beyond her years
- William J. Todd—Professor of the Practice, Georgia Institute of Technology
- Lamar Wright—Atlanta businessman and lifelong friend
- Amy Crownover—The editor and friend who kept things on track

And especially Kathy—my wife, my love and my best friend

Front Cover Photo: Thinkstock
Back Cover Photo: Michael Thompson, Micael-Renee' Lifestyle Portraiture, by permission